187225

PowerKids Readers:

The Bilingual Library of the United States of America™

Bilingual Edition
English/Spanish
Edición bilingüe

LOUISIANA
LUISIANA

VANESSA BROWN

TRADUCCIÓN AL ESPAÑOL: MARÍA CRISTINA BRUSCA

The Rosen Publishing Group's
PowerKids Press™ & **Editorial Buenas Letras**™
New York

Published in 2006 by The Rosen Publishing Group, Inc.
29 East 21st Street, New York, NY 10010

First Edition

Book Design: Albert B. Hanner

Photo Credits: Cover, p. 9 © Robert Holmes/Corbis; pp. 5, 30 (State Motto) Albert B. Hanner; p. 7 © 2002 Geoatlas; pp. 11, 15, 17, 31 (Long, Armstrong) © Bettman/Corbis; pp. 19, 23, 25, 30 (Capital), 31 (Silt) © Philip Gould/Corbis; pp. 21, 31 (Carnival) © Nathan Benn/Corbis; pp. 26, 30 (Bald Cypruss) © David Muench/Corbis; p. 30 (Magnolia) © Mark Bolton/Corbis; p. 30 (Eastern Brown Pelican) © Arthur Morris/Corbis; p. 30 (The Pelican State) © Dan Guravich/Corbis; p. 30 (Agate) © Peter Johnson/Corbis; p. 31 (Hellman) © Oscar White/Corbis; p. 31 (Jackson) © Underwood & Underwood/Corbis; p. 31 (Capote) © Hulton-Deutsch Collection/Corbis; p. 31 (Marsalis) © Lynn Goldsmith/Corbis; p. 31 (Wetland) © W. Cody/Corbis

Library of Congress Cataloging-in-Publication Data

Brown, Vanessa, 1963–
Louisiana / Vanessa Brown ; traducción al español, María Cristina Brusca.—1st ed.
p. cm. — (The bilingual library of the United States of America) Includes bibliographical references (p.) and index.
ISBN 1-4042-3083-1 (library bindings)
1. Louisiana–Juvenile literature. I. Title. II. Series.
F369.3.B76 2006
976.3—dc22
                                                    2005006103

Manufactured in the United States of America

Due to the changing nature of Internet links, Editorial Buenas Letras has developed an online list of Web sites related to the subject of this book. This site is updated regularly. Please use this link to access the list:

http://www.buenasletraslinks.com/ls/louisiana

Contents

Contenido

Welcome to Louisiana

These are the flag and seal of the state of Louisiana. The flag and seal show an eastern brown pelican, the state bird. Louisiana is known as the Pelican State.

Bienvenidos a Luisiana

Estos son la bandera y el escudo del estado de Luisiana. La bandera y el escudo muestran el ave del estado, el pelícano oriental marrón. Luisiana es conocido como el Estado del Pelícano.

UNION, JUSTICE & CONFIDENCE

STATE OF LOUISIANA · UNION · JUSTICE · CONFIDENCE

Louisiana Flag and State Seal

Bandera y escudo de Luisiana

Louisiana Geography

Louisiana borders the states of Mississippi, Arkansas, and Texas. Louisiana also borders the Gulf of Mexico. The Mississippi River forms part of the eastern border of the state.

Geografía de Luisiana

Luisiana linda con los estados de Misisipi, Arkansas y Texas. Luisiana también linda con el Golfo de México. El río Misisipi forma parte de la frontera oriental del estado.

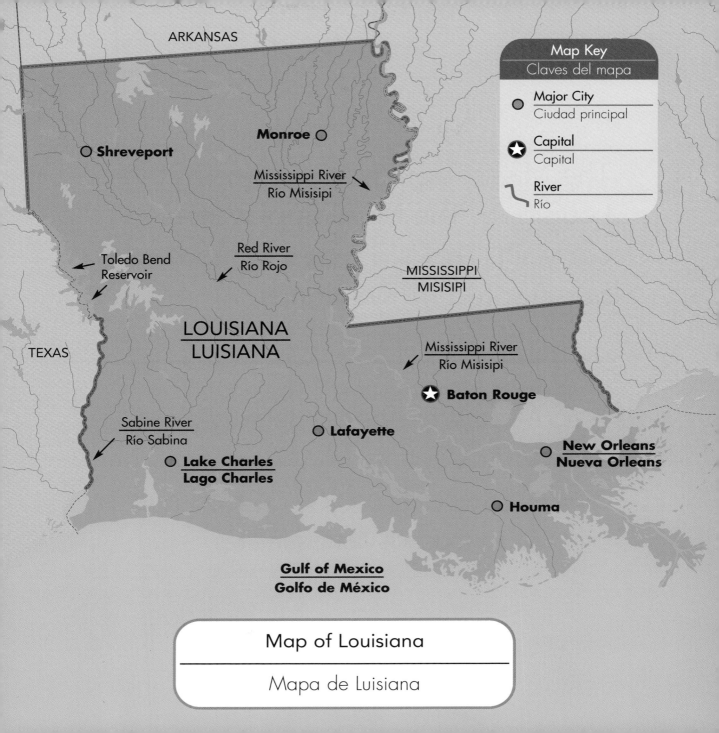

Map of Louisiana

Mapa de Luisiana

The Mississippi River is important for Louisiana. The Mississippi waters carry silt. This is a type of mud that has created rich wetlands.

El río Misisipi es importante para Luisiana. Las aguas del Misisipi arrastran cieno. El cieno es un tipo de lodo que ha creado muchas tierras fértiles.

A Mississippi Riverbank

Orillas del río Misisipi

Louisiana History

In 1682, French explorer René-Robert Cavelier de La Salle sailed the Mississippi River. La Salle claimed the land for France. He named it Louisiana to honor the French king, Louis XIV.

Historia de Luisiana

En 1682, el explorador francés René-Robert Cavalier de La Salle navegó por el río Misisipi. La Salle reclamó el territorio para Francia. Lo llamó Luisiana en honor al rey de Francia, Luis XIV.

La Salle Taking Control of Louisiana

La Salle toma posesión de Luisiana

American president Thomas Jefferson bought the Louisiana Territory from France in 1803. This deal is known as the Louisiana Purchase. It doubled the size of the United States.

En 1803, el presidente de los Estados Unidos, Thomas Jefferson le compró a Francia el Territorio de Luisiana. Este contrato se conoce como la Compra de Luisiana. El contrato duplicó el tamaño de los Estados Unidos.

The United States of America in 1803
Los Estados Unidos de América en 1803

Louisiana
Territory
Territorio de
Luisiana

Present-day Louisiana
Luisiana en la actualidad

Huey P. Long was Louisiana's governor from 1928 to 1932. Governor Long worked hard to make schools better. He also helped the poorest people of Louisiana.

Huey P. Long fue gobernador de Luisiana desde 1928 hasta 1932. El gobernador Long trabajó mucho para mejorar las escuelas. Long también ayudó a la gente más pobre de Luisiana.

Huey P. Long in 1935

Huey P. Long en 1935

In the 1960s, Louisiana's black students could not go to the same schools as white children. People fought against this. On November 14, 1960, Ruby Nell Bridges became the first African American child to go to a school with white students.

En los años 1960, los alumnos negros de Luisiana no podían asistir a las mismas escuelas que los niños blancos. Las personas lucharon en contra de estas reglas. El 14 de noviembre de 1960, Ruby Nell Bridges fue la primera niña afroamericana en asistir a la escuela junto a estudiantes blancos.

Ruby Nell Bridges at Age 6

Ruby Nell Bridges a la edad de 6 años

Living in Louisiana

Many Louisianans are Cajun. Cajuns come from French Canadians that moved to the state from Canada. Another group are Creole. Creoles have French, Spanish, African, and Caribbean origin.

La vida en Luisiana

Muchos luisianos tienen origen *cajun*. Los cajuns provienen de los franco-canadienses que se mudaron al estado desde Canadá. Otro gupo son *creole*. Los *creoles* tienen orígenes franceses, españoles, africanos y caribeños.

Cajun and Creole Citizens in Louisiana

Ciudadanos *cajuns* y *creoles* en Luisiana

Louisiana celebrates Mardi Gras with big carnivals. A carnival is a public celebration with rides and parades. The largest parade takes place in the city of New Orleans.

Luisiana celebra el Mardi Gras con grandes carnavales. Un carnaval es una celebración pública que incluye desfiles de carrozas. El desfile más grande tiene lugar en la ciudad de Nueva Orleans.

Parade at Mardi Gras
_____
Desfile de Mardi Gras

Louisiana is famous for its music. Music styles like jazz and blues started in the state. The New Orleans Jazz and Heritage Festival receives thousands of visitors every year.

Luisiana es famoso por su música. En este estado nacieron estilos musicales como el jazz y el blues. Todos los años, miles de visitantes acuden al Festival del Jazz y de la Tradición de Nueva Orleans.

Dancing in the Street During
the New Orleans Jazz and Heritage Festival

Bailes en la calle durante el Festival del Jazz y de
la Tradición de Nueva Orleans

New Orleans, Baton Rouge, Shreveport, Lafayette, and Monroe are important cities in Louisiana. Baton Rouge is the capital of the state.

Nueva Orleans, Baton Rouge, Shreveport, Lafayette y Monroe son ciudades importantes de Luisiana. Baton Rouge es la capital del estado.

Louisiana State Capitol Building in Baton Rouge

Capitolio del estado de Luisiana en Baton Rouge

Activity:
Let's Draw Louisiana's State Tree
The bald cypress became Louisiana's state tree in 1963.

Actividad:
Dibujemos el árbol del estado de Luisiana
El ciprés calvo es el árbol del estado de Luisiana desde 1963.

1

Start by drawing a tall rectangle.

Comienza por dibujar un rectángulo alto.

2

Inside the rectangle draw the outline of the top of the tree.

Traza el esquema de la copa del árbol adento del rectángulo.

3

Next draw the trunk, or bottom half of the tree. Add some of the branches.

Luego, dibuja el tronco o parte inferior del árbol.

4

Erase extra lines. Inside the shape for the top of the tree, draw in the leaves.

Dibuja las líneas innecesarias. Dibuja las hojas adentro de la forma de la copa.

5

Finish by shading the cypress tree.

Termina tu dibujo sombreando el ciprés.

Timeline

Cronología

Timeline		Cronología
Hernando de Soto becomes the first European to sail the Mississippi.	**1541**	Hernando de Soto es el primer europeo en navegar el río Misisipi.
René-Robert Cavelier de La Salle claims the Louisiana Territory for France.	**1682**	René-Robert Cavelier de La Salle reclama para Francia el Territorio de Luisiana.
The United States buys the Louisiana Territory from France.	**1803**	Los Estados Unidos le compran a Francia el Territorio de Luisiana.
Louisiana becomes the eighteenth state of the Union.	**1812**	Luisiana se convierte en el estado dieciocho de la Unión.
Baton Rouge becomes the capital of Louisiana.	**1849**	Baton Rouge pasa a ser la capital de Luisiana.
Oil deposits are found in Louisiana.	**1901**	Se encuentran yacimientos de petróleo en Luisiana.
The worst flood in U.S. history leaves 300,000 people homeless.	**1927**	La peor inundación de la historia de los E.U.A. deja sin hogar a 300,000 personas.

Louisiana Events

January
Sugar Bowl Football Game
in New Orleans

February
Mardi Gras festivities around the state

March
Taste of the Bayou Food Festival
in Houma

May
New Orleans Jazz and
Heritage Festival

June
Louisiana Peach Festival in Ruston

September
Festival Acadiens in Lafayette

October
Louisiana State Fair

December
Bonfires in the Mississippi River Levee

Eventos en Luisiana

Enero
Tazón del Azúcar, juego de fútbol
americano en Nueva Orleans

Febrero
Celebraciones de Mardi Gras, en todo
el estado

Marzo
Festival del sabor de la cocina de Bayou,
en Houma

Mayo
Festival del jazz y de la tradición de
Nueva Orleans

Junio
Festival del durazno de Luisiana,
en Ruston

Septiembre
Festival Acadiens en Lafayette

Octubre
Feria del estado de Luisiana

Diciembre
Fogatas en el malecón del río Misisipi

Louisiana Facts/Datos sobre Louisiana

Population
4.4 million

Población
4.4 millones

Capital
Baton Rouge

Capital
Baton Rouge

State Motto
Union, Justice and
Confidence

Lema del estado
Unión, justicia y
confianza

State Flower
Magnolia

Flor del estado
Magnolia

State Bird
Eastern brown
pelican

Ave del estado
Pelícano oriental
marrón

State Nickname
The Pelican State

Mote del estado
El Estado del Pelícano

State Tree
Bald cypress

Árbol del estado
Ciprés calvo

State Song
"Give Me Louisiana"

Canción del estado
"Dame Luisiana"

State Gemstone
Agate

Piedra preciosa
Ágata

Famous Louisianans/Liusianos famosos

Huey P. Long
(1893–1935)

Politician
Político

Louis Armstrong
(1900–1971)

Musician
Músico

Lillian Hellman
(1905–1984)

Playwright
Dramaturga

Mahalia Jackson
(1911–1972)

Gospel singer
Cantante de gospel

Truman Capote
(1924–1984)

Author
Escritor

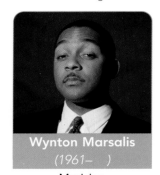

Wynton Marsalis
(1961–   )

Musician
Músico

Words to Know/Palabras que debes saber

border
frontera

carnival
carnaval

silt
cieno

wetland
tierras húmedas
y fértiles

31

Here are more books to read about Louisiana:
Otros libros que puedes leer sobre Luisiana:

In English/En inglés:

How to Draw Louisiana's Sights and Symbols
A Kid's Guide to Drawing America
by Deinard, Jenny
PowerKids Press, 2002

Louisiana
America the Beautiful
Second Series
by Hintz, Martin
Children's Press, 1998

Words in English: 320

Palabras en español: 363

Index

Índice